CONTENTS

Whether you're just beginning to master the perfect omelet or planning to cater your college reunion, quality equipment is key—which is why Jenn-Air has designed state-of-the-art accessories for its Expressions and Designer Line cooktops and ranges. These high-performance, interchangeable accessories are custom-tailored to accommodate your various needs. Switch between the grill and griddle, or add a rotiss-kebab or cooker-steamer, depending on the model you own. These elements allow you to grill a juicy burger, whip up delicious buttermilk pancakes, roast an elegant honey-glazed duck, and steam a basket of succulent seafood. In addition, they make it easier than ever to maintain a well-balanced diet by providing cooking methods that require little or no added fat.

On these pages you'll find an array of recipes that make the most of your Jenn-Air accessories. Adapted from international cuisines, many of the dishes use marinades or herb rubs that infuse foods with astonishing flavor. For variety and excitement, we've included interesting toppings like balsamic onions and vegetable slaw. There's also a great selection of hors d'oeuvres and appetizers, and you'll love the sweet treats you can cook on your griddle. The hardest part of using these versatile accessories is deciding what to make first.

On the cover: Honey-Mustard Shrimp, and Grilled Vegetables in Chianti-Herb Marinade. For recipes, see index.

Follow these basic tips to start using your grilling attachment for everything from hors d'oeuvres to hearty main course fare.

• Season grill grates when recipe specifies by brushing lightly with vegetable oil or spraying with nonstick cooking spray.

• Preheat on HI for five minutes after seasoning grates before placing food on grill to cook; preheating helps to sear the meat and retain foods' natural juices. Be sure the seasoned grates are in place while grill is preheating. Consult recipes and reduce grill heat to cook setting, if necessary. Just as with safe outdoor grilling, avoid wearing dangling jewelry and clothing with loose or wide sleeves while cooking.

• Choose meats that are cut at least ¾-inch thick for best grilling. Thinner-sliced meats, such as skinless, boneless chicken breasts, turkey, and veal cutlets are fine, but they cook quickly, so watch them carefully to be sure they do not become dry or overdone. Follow recipes carefully. For healthier cooking and to reduce excess smoke and flare-ups on the grill, always trim excess fat from meats.

• Place food on the grill with enough space between items for proper airflow. This allows for perfect doneness.

• Baste food sparingly during cooking. More is not better: excess liquid will only end up inside the grill.

• Turn meats with tongs. Never use a fork, which pierces the meat, causing it to lose valuable natural juices.

• Salt meats after cooking, never before; adding salt during cooking toughens the meat.

MARINADES

Whether you crave flavors that are spicy or delicate, a good marinade can satisfy your preference while adding valuable moisture to meats and poultry; it can even act as a light sauce. In addition, the acidic ingredients in marinades help tenderize foods, making them irresistibly succulent. For some basic standbys, follow the chart on the next page. A good rule of thumb is to allow a half cup of marinade for each pound of meat, and marinate four to six hours or overnight, depending upon the strength of

flavor desired. (There is one exception: Marinate fish no longer than two hours; if left longer, acids will "cook" the fish.) Marinate foods in a covered bowl or baking dish, as specified in recipe instructions. For even easier cleanup, place marinade in a zip-top plastic bag, add the meat or fish, and seal bag well, pressing out any excess air. To ensure that food is thoroughly coated, turn the contents of the bowl or occasionally shake the plastic bag.

SAFE MARINATING

Marinades can be a source of harmful bacteria if the proper handling techniques are ignored. For safe handling, follow these tips while marinating meats and fish.

• Let cooked marinade mixtures cool before using.

• Always marinate foods in the refrigerator, never at room temperature. If marinade has been left sitting out, do not brush it on food during the last five minutes of cooking, as this is not enough time for the heat to destroy any harmful bacteria.

• Do not reuse plates or utensils that have held raw foods; place cooked food on a clean plate.

• Never use leftover marinade unless it has been brought to a boil for one minute. This will kill any bacteria transferred from the raw meat juices.

TYPE	INGREDIENTS AND PROCEDURE	BEST USED ON
Curry (1 cup)	1½ teaspoons curry powder, 1 teaspoon sugar, ¼ teaspoon ground nutmeg, ⅓ cup soy sauce, ¼ cup lemon juice, ¼ cup vegetable oil, 3 tablespoons water, 1 tablespoon honey, 1 clove garlic (minced) *Combine all ingredients in small saucepan and heat to boiling, stirring constantly. Reduce heat; cover. Simmer five minutes, stirring occasionally. Cool.*	Beef Chicken Lamb Pork
Garlic-Dill Butter* (¾ cup)	1 large clove garlic (quartered), ½ cup butter, ¼ teaspoon lemon pepper, ½ teaspoon dried dill *Melt butter in small saucepan and sauté garlic; when garlic is browned, remove and discard it. Stir in remaining ingredients.*	Fish Seafood
Indian (1 cup)	1 cup plain yogurt, 1 tablespoon vegetable oil, 1 tablespoon tomato paste, 2 cloves garlic (peeled and crushed through a press), 1 teaspoon each ground ginger and coriander, ½ teaspoon ground turmeric, ½ teaspoon chili powder, ¼ teaspoon ground cinnamon *Whisk all ingredients together until well combined.*	Chicken Pork Tenderloin Turkey
Italian Herb (About ⅔ cup)	⅓ cup red wine, ¼ cup olive oil, 1 tablespoon lemon juice, 1 clove garlic (peeled and crushed through a press), 2 teaspoons mixed dried Italian herbs (thyme, oregano, basil, and rosemary), ¼ teaspoon crushed red pepper flakes, salt and pepper to taste *Whisk all ingredients together until well combined.*	Beef (steaks) Chicken (skinless, boneless) Fish Vegetables
Polynesian (1 cup)	¾ cup pineapple juice, ¼ cup mango chutney, 1 tablespoon vegetable oil, 2 teaspoons cider vinegar or dry sherry, 1 teaspoon Worcestershire sauce, ½ teaspoon ground ginger *Combine all ingredients in small saucepan; cook over medium heat until heated through, about two minutes.*	Beef Chicken Pork Shrimp
Red Wine* (About 1¼ cups)	½ cup dry red wine, ½ cup water, 3 tablespoons coarsely chopped onion, 1 clove garlic (quartered), 3 tablespoons lime juice, 2 tablespoons packed brown sugar, ½ tablespoon salt *Combine all ingredients; heat to boiling, stirring constantly. Reduce heat; cover. Simmer five minutes, stirring occasionally. Discard garlic and let marinade cool. Variation: Substitute 1 can (10½ ounces) beef broth for the wine and water.*	Beef
Teriyaki* (¾ cup)	¼ cup water, ¼ cup soy sauce, 2 tablespoons dry sherry, 1 tablespoon sesame oil, 2 tablespoons packed brown sugar, ¼ cup chopped green onion, 1 clove garlic (quartered), ½ teaspoon minced fresh ginger *Combine all ingredients in a small saucepan; heat to boiling, stirring constantly. Reduce heat; cover. Simmer five minutes, stirring occasionally. Discard garlic and let marinade cool.*	Beef Chicken Fish Pork
White Wine* (¾ cup)	½ cup dry white wine, ¼ cup olive oil, 1 teaspoon dried basil or oregano, 1 teaspoon Worcestershire sauce, ¼ teaspoon salt, ¼ teaspoon coarsely ground pepper, ⅛ teaspoon garlic powder *Combine all ingredients in small mixing bowl. Variation: Substitute 1 teaspoon dried rosemary or dried tarragon for the basil.*	Beef Chicken Fish Lamb Pork

* These marinades can be used immediately by simply brushing on food while grilling.

Recipes for the GRILL

Using the grill accessory rewards you with juicy, full-flavored foods that have authentic grilled taste in any weather. And no more fussing with messy charcoal. Even when you crave your summertime favorites in the middle of winter, this attachment lets you enjoy their rich, smoked flavor in minutes. And it's not just for burgers and steaks—these creative recipes will add flair to any meal. Jenn-Air's specially designed ventilation system pulls smoke across the food and away from you, while the precisely calibrated heat settings cook foods to perfection every time. For safe and easy grilling, review the tips on page 2.

Spinach and Cheese Stuffed Pizzas

Prepackaged pizza dough makes these crusty, grilled surprise packages an easy lunchtime favorite for kids.

2 garlic cloves, crushed through a press
¼ cup olive oil
1 package (10 ounces) frozen spinach, thawed and squeezed dry
¼ teaspoon salt
⅛ teaspoon pepper
1 package (10 ounces) prepared pizza dough
3 ounces (about ½ cup) goat cheese, crumbled, or mozzarella, shredded
¼ cup sun-dried tomatoes
2 tablespoons chopped fresh basil
½ teaspoon red pepper flakes

In small bowl, combine garlic and olive oil; in a separate bowl, season spinach with salt and pepper. Set both aside.

On lightly floured surface, roll out dough to ⅛-inch thickness, forming a 12- by 16-inch rectangle; then cut dough in half, forming two 12- by 8-inch rectangles. Brush dough with garlic oil, leaving a ¾-inch border all around. Divide spinach, cheese, sun-dried tomatoes, basil, and red pepper flakes, and sprinkle on half of each rectangle. Stretch the uncovered portions of dough over fillings and press to close, pressing out excess air. Crimp edges with a fork to seal well. Turn the pizzas, crimp again, and brush the tops with garlic oil. Season grill grates; preheat on HI for 5 minutes, then reduce to appropriate cook setting.

Place pizzas on grill, oiled sides down. Brush tops with oil. Cook 12 to 16 minutes, turning and rotating the pizzas every 4 to 5 minutes (on Designer gas model, first turn should be after 2 to 3 minutes). Remove pizzas when they are golden brown; brush with additional oil, if desired. Let cool slightly; to serve, cut each into 4 triangles.

Makes 8 servings

	Preheat	Setting	Time
Electric	HI	8	16
Gas	HI	LO	12

Spinach and Cheese Stuffed Pizzas

Barbecued Sweet Potatoes

Easy Indonesian **Satay**

In southeast Asian cuisines, a spicy peanut dipping sauce often accompanies these strips of skewered meat. Here, the same flavors are used in a delicious marinade.

- ½ cup creamy-style peanut butter
- ¼ cup soy sauce
- ¼ cup honey
- 2 tablespoons rice vinegar
- 2 tablespoons freshly squeezed lime juice
- 2 tablespoons minced green onions, white parts only
- 2 tablespoons water
- 2 tablespoons sesame oil
- 2 tablespoons shredded fresh ginger
- 1 teaspoon curry powder
- 2 garlic cloves, crushed through a press
- ½ teaspoon cayenne pepper, or to taste
- 1 pound skinless, boneless chicken breasts, cut into thin strips ½-inch wide
- 12 to 16 bamboo skewers (12-inch size), soaked in water for 30 minutes

To make marinade, in medium bowl, whisk together all ingredients, except chicken, until smooth. Reserve half of the marinade for use as the dipping sauce.

Add chicken strips to marinade. Cover bowl and refrigerate 1 hour, turning chicken occasionally.

Thread 1 chicken strip, accordion-style, onto each of the skewers to within an inch of skewer end.

Season grill grates; preheat on HI for 5 minutes. Place skewers on grill, being careful not to overcrowd. Grill 6 to 8 minutes or until chicken is cooked through, turning frequently.

Serve with the remaining dipping sauce.   **Makes 12 to 16 appetizers**

	Preheat	Setting	Time
Electric	HI	HI	6 to 8
Gas	HI	HI	6 to 8

Thai Grilled **Chicken Wings**

Watch these disappear at your next party—and keep this easy marinade recipe handy for use with other cuts of chicken as well.

- 1½ pounds chicken wings
- ½ cup water
- ¼ cup soy sauce
- ¼ cup Worcestershire sauce
- Grated zest of 1 lime
- Juice of 1 lime
- 2 tablespoons fresh ginger, minced
- 1 tablespoon sugar
- 3 garlic cloves, minced
- ¼ teaspoon crushed hot red pepper flakes

With a heavy cleaver or large knife, cut off wing tips at joints and discard. Cut each of the remaining wings into two pieces at joint.

To make marinade, combine all remaining ingredients in a bowl. Add the chicken wings and toss well to coat. Cover bowl and refrigerate at least 4 hours, preferably overnight, turning chicken occasionally.

Season grill grates; preheat on HI for 5 minutes, then reduce to appropriate cook setting.

Grill chicken wings thoroughly, 16 to 20 minutes, turning often. Brush with marinade occasionally, if desired, but not during the last 5 minutes of cooking.   **Makes about 20 appetizers**

	Preheat	Setting	Time
Electric	HI	10	16 to 20
Gas	HI	MED	16 to 20

Sausage and Pear **Kebabs**

This unexpected combination creates a hearty autumn appetizer. When pears are at their peak, their crunchy sweetness contrasts nicely with the spiciness of sausage.

- 1 pound sweet Italian pork or turkey sausage (about 6 links), pierced with a fork
- 2 firm, ripe Bosc pears (about 1 pound), peeled and cored
- 1 tablespoon freshly squeezed lemon juice
- ¼ teaspoon ground fennel seeds
- ¼ teaspoon freshly ground pepper
- 24 bamboo skewers (6-inch size), soaked in water for 30 minutes

Place sausage in large skillet; add enough water to cover, and bring to a boil over high heat. Reduce heat to 6 (for Designer gas model, use MED) and simmer until sausage is partly cooked, about 7 minutes. Turn halfway through cooking time. Remove sausage from heat and cut each link into 4 rounds.

Quarter the pears and cut each quarter into three pieces. In medium bowl, toss pear chunks with lemon juice, ground fennel seeds, and pepper. Alternately thread one piece of sausage, lollipop-style, and one chunk of pear onto each skewer to within an inch of skewer tips.

Season grill grates; preheat on HI for 5 minutes, then reduce to appropriate cook setting. Grill kebabs 10 to 12 minutes, or until sausage is browned, turning after half the time.   **Makes 24 appetizers**

	Preheat	Setting	Time
Electric	HI	10	10 to 12
Gas	HI	MED	10 to 12

Honey-Mustard **Shrimp**

Tangy and sweet, this is finger food at its best. The shrimp are a perfect accompaniment to wine or cocktails at a party, but they also make a terrific first course at dinner.

2 tablespoons honey
2 tablespoons Dijon mustard
2 tablespoons freshly squeezed lemon juice
1½ tablespoons shallots or green onions, green and white parts, chopped
1 tablespoon fresh rosemary, chopped, or 1 teaspoon dried
¼ teaspoon salt
⅛ teaspoon freshly ground pepper
¼ cup vegetable oil
1 pound (22 to 25) medium shrimp, peeled and deveined
22 to 25 bamboo skewers (12-inch size), soaked in water for 30 minutes

To make marinade, combine all ingredients except oil and shrimp in medium bowl. Using a wire whisk, gradually add oil until mixture thickens. Add shrimp and toss well to coat thoroughly; cover and refrigerate 1 to 2 hours.

Season grill grates; preheat on HI for 5 minutes, then reduce to appropriate cook setting. Shake excess marinade from shrimp. Thread the top and bottom of each shrimp onto a bamboo skewer, being sure each maintains its natural curve, as shown. Grill 5 to 10 minutes or until shrimp is firm and pink, basting with marinade if desired and turning after half the cooking time.

Makes about 24 appetizers

	Preheat	Setting	Time
Electric	HI	10	5 to 10
Gas	HI	MED	5 to 10

Gorgonzola and Walnut **Bruschetta**

Italian bruschetta—little rounds of grilled bread with an array of delicious toppings, are just the thing to serve with wine or cocktails before a dinner party. As a variation, top the toasts with thinly sliced pears or apples before adding the gorgonzola.

8 ounces blue cheese (preferably gorgonzola) at room temperature
2 tablespoons port wine
¼ teaspoon freshly ground pepper
30 slices French or Italian bread from a 3-inch-diameter loaf, cut ¼-inch thick
½ cup finely chopped walnuts

In small bowl, mash cheese with a fork; mix in the port wine and pepper, and stir until smooth. Set aside.

Preheat grill on HI for 5 minutes, then adjust to appropriate cook setting. Grill bread for about 2 minutes, or until lightly toasted on both sides, turning halfway through cooking time. While toasts are warm, spread each with about 1 teaspoon of the cheese mixture and sprinkle with walnuts. Serve immediately.

Makes 30 toasts

	Preheat	Setting	Time
Electric	HI	10	2
Gas	HI	HI	2

Korean-Style
Marinated Beef

In Korean cuisine, this robust marinade is used for many kinds of meat, including chicken and pork. To make this dish a meal, serve with bowls of steamed rice.

1 tablespoon sesame seeds

⅓ cup soy sauce

2 shallots or green onions, white and green parts, finely chopped

1 tablespoon light brown sugar

1 tablespoon sesame oil or vegetable oil

1 tablespoon fresh ginger, minced

¼ teaspoon crushed hot red pepper flakes

1½ pounds boneless beef sirloin steak, cut about ¾-inch thick

Buttercrunch or red leaf lettuce leaves, rinsed and dried

1 red onion, thinly sliced

Hoisin sauce

In a medium skillet, toast sesame seeds at setting 6 (for Designer gas model, use MED), stirring constantly, about 6 minutes. Transfer to a shallow baking dish. Add soy sauce, green onions, brown sugar, oil, ginger, and red pepper; mix well. Score fat along the edge of the steak to prevent curling while cooking. Place steak in baking dish and turn to coat with marinade. Cover dish and refrigerate at least 4 hours, preferably overnight, turning steak occasionally.

Season grill grates; preheat on HI for 5 minutes. Grill steak 10 to 20 minutes, or until rare to medium, as desired. Turn after half the cooking time, brushing frequently with marinade. Remove steak from grill; set aside for 5 minutes before slicing.

To serve, cut steak diagonally into thin slices and transfer to a platter. Each person places a few slices of the beef, along with juices, in a lettuce leaf, adds onion and hoisin sauce to taste, then folds up the lettuce leaf to form a small packet. *Makes 4 to 6 servings*

	Preheat	Setting	Time
Electric	HI	HI	12 to 20
Gas	HI	HI	10 to 16

Caribbean Jerk Pork

In Jamaica, meat is marinated in a hotter-than-hot paste, then grilled and "jerked" apart into pieces. Even though this pork tenderloin is sliced rather than shredded, the flavor is authentic, heady with green onions, allspice, chili, and fruit juice.

¼ cup vegetable oil

2 tablespoons dark rum

2 tablespoons honey

Juice of two limes

4 green onions, chopped

4 garlic cloves, crushed

2 tablespoons fresh ginger, grated

1 small hot chili pepper, seeded and chopped

1 teaspoon ground allspice

1 teaspoon ground cinnamon

1 teaspoon ground nutmeg

½ teaspoon salt

¼ teaspoon freshly ground pepper

1½ pounds boneless pork tenderloin, trimmed of silverskin

In a medium bowl, combine all ingredients except pork. Add pork, cover bowl, and marinate at least 4 hours or overnight, turning pork occasionally.

Season grill grates; preheat on HI for 5 minutes, then adjust to appropriate cook setting. Cook 30 to 40 minutes, or until meat is cooked through (160° on a meat thermometer), turning every 5 minutes. Set aside for 5 minutes before cutting into thin, diagonal slices to serve.

Makes 6 servings

	Preheat	Setting	Time
Electric	HI	10	30 to 40
Gas	HI	MED	30 to 40

Pork Chops in Herbed
Sweet Brine

A sugar-enhanced brine infuses the pork with truly surprising flavor but none of the acidity often found in marinades. Try this method—you'll be convinced.

10 cups water

3 tablespoons salt, preferably noniodized

⅓ cup sugar

1 teaspoon dried rosemary

1 teaspoon dried sage

1 teaspoon dried thyme

3 bay leaves

1 teaspoon whole black peppercorns

2 tablespoons gin, optional

4 center-cut loin chops (about 2 pounds), cut 1-inch thick

In large saucepan, bring water plus the sugar, salt, and spices to a simmer; cook over low heat 15 minutes. Let cool completely. Stir in gin, if desired. Transfer brine to a glass or enamel bowl.

Score fat around edges of pork chops to prevent curling during cooking. Place chops in brine; cover and refrigerate 12 to 24 hours. Remove chops from brine, scrape off herbs, and pat dry with paper towels.

Season grill grates; preheat on HI for 5 minutes, then reduce to appropriate cook setting. Turning every five minutes or so, grill pork chops 30 to 40 minutes, or until meat shows no trace of pink when pierced at the bone with a knife. *Makes 4 servings*

	Preheat	Setting	Time
Electric	HI	10	30 to 40
Gas	HI	MED	30 to 40

Korean-Style Marinated Beef

Leg of Lamb with Provençal Herb Rub

This aromatic blend of regional French herbs is the traditional complement to leg of lamb cooked in the French manner.

- 1 teaspoon dried rosemary
- ½ teaspoon dried thyme
- ½ teaspoon dried basil
- ½ teaspoon dried savory or marjoram
- ½ teaspoon salt
- ¼ teaspoon dried, crushed lavender, optional (available at some natural food stores)
- ¼ teaspoon pepper
- 1 tablespoon olive oil
- 2 garlic cloves, crushed through a press
- 4 leg of lamb steaks, cut ¾-inch thick

To make the Provençal herb rub, combine dry ingredients in a small bowl, crushing them between your fingers as you mix.

In another small bowl, combine oil and garlic. Score any fat along the edges of steaks to prevent curling while cooking. Brush both sides of lamb steaks with the garlic oil, then rub in the herb mixture. Place lamb on a plate, cover, and refrigerate 1 hour.

Season grill grates; preheat grill on HI for 5 minutes, then reduce to appropriate cook setting. Grill steaks 20 to 30 minutes, turning every 5 minutes.

Set steaks aside for 5 minutes before serving. Makes 4 servings

	Preheat	Setting	Time
Electric	HI	10	20 to 30
Gas	HI	MED	20 to 25

Pork Spareribs with Peach-Bourbon Glaze

Here's a new twist on an old favorite: A bourbon-laced, peachy-peppery glaze is brushed on the ribs during grilling.

- 1 cup water
- 1 teaspoon salt
- 1 medium onion, cut into quarters
- 4 pounds pork spareribs, cut into 2- or 3-rib sections
- 1 tablespoon paprika
- 1 teaspoon onion salt
- ½ teaspoon garlic powder
- ½ teaspoon freshly ground pepper
- 1 teaspoon cornstarch
- ¼ cup bourbon or apple juice
- 1 cup peach preserves
- 2 tablespoons butter or margarine
- 1 small hot chili pepper, seeded and minced

Pour water into a Dutch oven; stir in salt and add onion and spareribs. Boil, then reduce heat to setting 3 or 4 (for Designer gas model, use LO); simmer, covered, for 1½ to 2 hours, or until meat is tender. Remove ribs from liquid and let cool slightly.

In small bowl, combine paprika, onion salt, garlic powder, and pepper. Rub into spareribs and set aside for 30 minutes.

Meanwhile, make glaze. In small saucepan, dissolve cornstarch in bourbon. Add peach preserves, butter, and chili pepper; simmer over low heat until butter is melted and sauce thickens slightly, stirring often. Set glaze aside.

Season grill grates; preheat on HI for 5 minutes, then reduce to appropriate cook setting.

Brush ribs well with glaze and grill 12 to 20 minutes, or until nicely browned. Turn every 5 minutes, brushing often with glaze. Makes 4 servings

	Preheat	Setting	Time
Electric	HI	10	12 to 15
Gas	HI	MED	15 to 20

Hoisin Barbecued Flank Steak

In China, meats are often marinated in this aromatic sauce before grilling. Hoisin sauce and rice vinegar are Oriental cooking staples that are now widely available in the Asian food sections of many grocery stores.

- ½ cup hoisin sauce
- ¼ cup vegetable oil
- ¼ cup rice wine vinegar
- ¼ cup dry sherry
- 2 tablespoons soy sauce
- 2 tablespoons honey
- 2 tablespoons grated fresh ginger
- 1 teaspoon sesame oil
- 1 green onion, white and green parts, finely chopped
- 1 garlic clove, crushed through a press
- ½ teaspoon crushed hot red pepper flakes
- 1¼ pounds flank steak

In large baking dish, combine all ingredients except steak. Add steak, cover, and refrigerate at least 8 hours, turning occasionally.

Season grill grates; preheat on HI for 5 minutes. Grill steak, brushing often

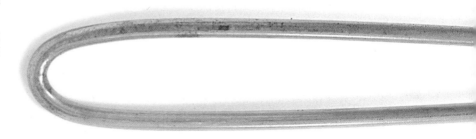

burgers

with the marinade, for 10 to 17 minutes or until medium-rare. Turn halfway through cooking time. Set steak aside for 5 minutes before cutting into thin diagonal slices.   Makes 4 to 6 servings

	Preheat	Setting	Time
Electric	HI	HI	13 to 17
Gas	HI	HI	10 to 12

T-Bone Steak Florentine

Here's a simple preparation for steak, the Tuscan way. Use fine-quality extra-virgin olive oil to enhance the flavor and capture the authentic taste. Steamed fresh spinach is a perfect accompaniment.

- 2 T-bone steaks (about 3 pounds), cut 1-inch thick and patted dry
- 4 teaspoons extra-virgin olive oil, divided
- Salt and freshly ground pepper to taste
- Lemon wedges

Season grill grates; preheat on HI for 5 minutes.

Drizzle ¼ teaspoon olive oil on both sides of each steak and rub into meat. Grill steaks 13 to 19 minutes for rare to medium-rare, as desired; turn after half the cooking time. Remove steaks from grill; season each on both sides with salt and pepper. Set aside and let rest for 5 minutes before serving.

Drizzle steaks with remaining olive oil and serve with lemon wedges.

Makes 2 servings

	Preheat	Setting	Time
Electric	HI	HI	13 to 19
Gas	HI	HI	14 to 18

Cheddar-Chutney Turkey Burgers

Ground turkey is now available in regular and extra-lean varieties. Extra-lean is great for sauces and casseroles, but for juicy burgers, go with regular ground turkey.

- 1¼ to 1⅓ pounds ground turkey
- ⅓ cup mango chutney, chopped
- 2 tablespoons bread crumbs
- ½ teaspoon salt
- ¼ teaspoon pepper
- 4 slices red onion, ¼-inch thick
- 1 teaspoon olive oil
- 4 slices sharp cheddar cheese
- 4 hamburger buns, split
- ¼ cup regular or low-fat mayonnaise
- ½ teaspoon curry powder
- Lettuce leaves and tomato slices, optional

In medium bowl, mix ground turkey, chutney, bread crumbs, salt, and pepper. Divide the mixture and shape into four patties, each ½- to ¾-inch thick.

Season grill grates; preheat on HI for 5 minutes, then adjust to appropriate cook setting. Grill burgers for 20 to 25 minutes, or until they are cooked through. Turn 2 or 3 times during cooking. Brush onion slices on both sides with olive oil and season with salt and pepper, if desired. Place on grill during last 10 minutes of burger cooking time and cook until onions are tender, turning once halfway through. During the last 3 to 5 minutes of cooking, top each burger with a slice of cheese. Place buns on grill and toast until golden.

Meanwhile, in a small bowl, combine mayonnaise and curry powder and spread on toasted buns. To serve, place burgers in buns, topping them with grilled onions, lettuce, and tomatoes, if desired.   Makes 4 servings

	Preheat	Setting	Time
Electric	HI	10	20 to 25
Gas	HI	MED	20 to 25

Meatloaf Burgers

It's the meatloaf you know and love, but in patty form it cooks up much faster than the traditional version.

- 6 ounces ground beef
- 6 ounces ground pork
- 6 ounces ground veal
- ¼ cup plain dry bread crumbs
- 3 tablespoons minced onion
- 2 tablespoons ketchup, plus additional ketchup for serving
- 1 tablespoon Worcestershire sauce
- Yolk of 1 egg
- ½ teaspoon salt
- ¼ teaspoon pepper
- 4 hamburger buns, split

In medium bowl, combine the ground meats, bread crumbs, onion, ketchup, Worcestershire sauce, egg yolk, salt, and pepper; shape into 4 patties, each ½- to ¾-inch thick.

Season grill grates; preheat on HI for 5 minutes, then reduce to appropriate cook setting. Cook patties 18 to 25 minutes, turning after half the cooking time. Toast buns during the last 2 to 3 minutes of cooking time, if desired. Serve on toasted buns with additional ketchup on the side.   Makes 4 servings

	Preheat	Setting	Time
Electric	HI	10	18 to 25
Gas	HI	MED	20 to 25

Veal Chops with Grilled
Pepper and Black Olive Salsa

Veal Chops with Grilled Pepper and Black Olive Salsa

Simple veal chops are treated to a robust dose of Mediterranean flavor with this savory and colorful salsa.

4 rib veal chops (about 2½ pounds), cut ¾-inch thick

1½ teaspoons fresh rosemary, chopped, or ½ teaspoon dried, crumbled

¾ teaspoon salt, divided

⅜ teaspoon freshly ground black pepper, divided

1 red bell pepper, seeded and quartered

1 yellow bell pepper, seeded and quartered

1 large red onion, cut into ½-inch slices

¼ cup balsamic vinegar

2 garlic cloves, minced

1 tablespoon chopped fresh basil

⅓ cup virgin olive oil

½ cup Mediterranean olives (Kalamata or oil-cured), pitted and chopped

Season veal with rosemary, ½ teaspoon salt, and ¼ teaspoon pepper; set aside.

Season grill grates; preheat on HI for 5 minutes. Place quartered red and yellow peppers on grill, skin side down; cook 20 to 25 minutes or until charred. Transfer to a brown paper bag, close tightly, and set bag aside for 10 minutes to allow steam to loosen skins. Meanwhile, grill onion slices for 10 minutes, turning after half the time. Set aside to cool.

Remove peppers from bag; peel off and discard the charred skins; rinse under running water and pat dry with paper towels. Slice peppers into thin strips.

To make the salsa, in small bowl, combine the vinegar, garlic, basil, ¼ teaspoon salt, and ⅛ teaspoon pepper. Slowly whisk in a thin stream of oil. Separate onion rings and add to mixture, along with pepper strips and chopped olives.

Grill veal chops 14 to 17 minutes, or until done, turning every 4 or 5 minutes.

Set aside for 5 minutes before serving.

To serve, place one veal chop on each plate and top with one quarter of the salsa mixture; drizzle with the liquid remaining in bowl.

Makes 4 servings

	Preheat	Setting	Time
Electric	HI	HI	15 to 17
Gas	HI	HI	14 to 16

Chicken Breasts with Afghani Yogurt Marinade

Yogurt is a popular marinade ingredient in Eastern cuisines. It creates a wonderfully tasty glaze on grilled meats and poultry.

¾ cup plain yogurt

1 small onion, coarsely chopped

¼ cup parsley, chopped

4 garlic cloves, crushed through a press

2 tablespoons freshly squeezed lemon juice

1 tablespoon olive oil

1½ teaspoons paprika

1 teaspoon dried oregano

1 teaspoon ground cumin

1 teaspoon salt

½ teaspoon cayenne pepper

4 skinless, boneless chicken breasts (about 6 ounces each)

Place all ingredients, except chicken, in blender or food processor, and mix until smooth. Pour into a baking dish. Add chicken; cover dish and refrigerate at least 4 hours, turning chicken occasionally.

Season grill grates; preheat on HI for 5 minutes, then reduce to appropriate cook setting. Grill chicken 25 to 35 minutes, or until cooked through, turning every 5 minutes.

Makes 4 servings

	Preheat	Setting	Time
Electric	HI	10	25 to 35
Gas	HI	MED	25 to 30

Turkey Breast Saltimbocca

In Italian, saltimbocca literally means "jump in the mouth," and that is exactly what the flavors in this recipe do. Elegant enough for a party yet easy enough for an everyday dinner, this dish is bound to become a favorite.

8 turkey breast cutlets (about 1½ pounds)

½ teaspoon salt

½ teaspoon pepper

2 teaspoons fresh sage, finely chopped, or 1 teaspoon dried sage, crumbled

6 ounces mozzarella, thinly sliced and cut to fit cutlets

2 ounces prosciutto, thinly sliced and cut to fit cutlets

2 tablespoons chopped parsley, optional

Lemon wedges, optional

Place turkey cutlets between two pieces of plastic wrap and gently pound to uniform thickness; season on both sides with salt and pepper.

Season grill grates; preheat on HI for 5 minutes, then reduce to appropriate cook setting. Place half of the cutlets on the grill and cook about 5 minutes, or just until undersides are done. Turn cutlets and top the cooked sides with half the sage, sliced mozzarella, and prosciutto. Cook about 5 minutes more. Transfer cutlets to a serving platter and keep warm. Repeat procedure with remaining four cutlets and topping ingredients.

Serve hot, sprinkled with chopped parsley and lemon wedges.

Makes 4 servings

	Preheat	Setting	Time
Electric	HI	10	9 to 12
Gas	HI	MED	9 to 12

Chicken Breasts in Lime Teriyaki

Now you can make your favorite Japanese dish at home. For juicy chicken breasts with less fat, leave the skin on during cooking and remove afterward.

½ cup soy sauce
¼ cup dry sherry
1 shallot or green onion, white and green parts, minced
Grated zest of 1 lime
3 tablespoons freshly squeezed lime juice
2 tablespoons minced fresh ginger
2 tablespoons brown sugar
¼ teaspoon pepper
4 chicken breast halves (about 2 pounds)

In medium baking dish, combine all ingredients except chicken. Add chicken, cover, and refrigerate 3 to 4 hours, turning chicken occasionally.

Season grill grates; preheat on HI for 5 minutes, then reduce to appropriate cook setting. Place chicken skin side down on grill and cook 40 to 55 minutes, or until meat is no longer pink, turning every 5 minutes. To serve, remove bones and reserve for another use. *Makes 4 servings*

	Preheat	Setting	Time
Electric	HI	10	45 to 55
Gas	HI	MED	40 to 50

Dijon Mustard–Coated Potatoes

New potatoes marinated in a zesty Dijon mustard mixture make an unbeatable side dish for grilled steaks. Parboiling the potatoes before grilling ensures tenderness.

15 small red potatoes (about 1½ pounds) scrubbed and cut in halves
½ cup Dijon mustard
¼ cup olive oil, preferably extra-virgin
¼ cup chopped shallots or green onions, white parts only
1 tablespoon chopped fresh rosemary, or 1 teaspoon dried
2 garlic cloves, crushed through a press
½ teaspoon salt
¼ teaspoon pepper

In large pot of boiling salted water, parboil potatoes over high heat about 12 minutes, or until barely tender. Drain. Meanwhile, combine all remaining ingredients in a large bowl. Add warm potatoes and toss well. Let cool. Cover bowl and refrigerate for 2 to 6 hours.

Season grill grates; preheat on HI for 5 minutes, then adjust to appropriate cook setting. Cook potatoes 15 to 20 minutes or until browned, turning often. *Makes 4 to 6 servings*

	Preheat	Setting	Time
Electric	HI	10	15 to 20
Gas	HI	HI	15 to 20

Barbecued Sweet Potatoes

These sweet potatoes are perfect with baked ham or grilled pork chops. You'll want to keep the barbecue sauce recipe close by for use with chicken and spareribs, too.

1 tablespoon vegetable oil
1 small onion, chopped
1 garlic clove, minced
½ cup ketchup
½ cup prepared chili sauce
¼ cup cider vinegar
¼ cup light brown sugar, firmly packed
1 tablespoon Worcestershire sauce
1 tablespoon prepared steak sauce
1 tablespoon spicy brown mustard
Hot red pepper sauce to taste
3 large (about 1¼ pound) sweet potatoes, scrubbed and unpeeled
Nonstick cooking spray

To make barbecue sauce, heat oil in medium saucepan at setting 6 (for Designer gas model, use MED). Add onion and garlic; cover. Cook about 6 minutes, or until onion is golden. Stir in ketchup, chili sauce, vinegar, brown sugar, Worcestershire and steak sauces, and mustard. Bring to a simmer; cook over low heat, stirring often to avoid scorching, about 45 minutes, or until mixture thickens slightly. Season with hot red pepper sauce to taste.

In a large pot of lightly salted boiling water, cook potatoes about 25 minutes, or until barely tender when pierced with a knife. Drain, rinse under cold water, and let cool. Cut lengthwise into quarters.

Season grill grates; preheat grill on HI for 5 minutes. Spray potatoes with nonstick cooking spray and place on grill. Cook for 10 to 12 minutes, basting with barbecue sauce and turning every 2 minutes or so, or until sauce is bubbly and glazed. Brush with additional sauce before serving, if desired. *Makes 4 servings*

	Preheat	Setting	Time
Electric	HI	HI	10 to 12
Gas	HI	HI	10

Grilled Swordfish Kebabs with Orange-Mint Marinade

These satisfying, chunky kebabs are infused with the aromatic flavor of bay leaves during cooking. Try this recipe with tuna chunks, too.

Juice of 1 orange

Juice of 1 lemon

Grated zest of 1 orange

Grated zest of 1 lemon

⅓ cup extra-virgin olive oil

1 tablespoon fresh mint, chopped, or 1 teaspoon dried

1 teaspoon dried oregano

1 garlic clove, crushed through a press

1½ pounds fresh swordfish, cut into 24 1-inch chunks

2 sweet red bell peppers, seeded and cut into 24 pieces

24 fresh bay leaves; if using dried bay leaves, soak in water for 5 minutes, then drain

6 bamboo skewers (12-inch size), soaked in water for 30 minutes

¼ teaspoon salt

⅛ teaspoon pepper

In a baking dish, combine orange and lemon juices and zests, oil, mint, oregano,

and garlic; add the swordfish. Cover dish and refrigerate no longer than 1 to 2 hours, turning the fish occasionally.

Alternately thread swordfish cubes, pepper pieces, and bay leaves onto skewers.

Season grill grates; preheat on HI for 5 minutes. Cook kebabs 15 to 18 minutes or until fish flakes easily with a fork, turning every 2 minutes. Remove kebabs from grill and season with salt and pepper to taste. Discard bay leaves before serving kebabs. *Makes 6 servings*

	Preheat	Setting	Time
Electric	HI	HI	15 to 18
Gas	HI	HI	15 to 18

Lobster Tails with Lemon-Herb Butter

Lobster tails are at their best when slathered with herb butter, then grilled. You can substitute dill or basil for the tarragon for a slightly different flavor.

4 raw lobster tails (6 to 8 ounces each)

2 sticks butter

½ cup freshly squeezed lemon juice

2 teaspoons chopped fresh tarragon, or 1 teaspoon dried

2 garlic cloves, minced

½ teaspoon salt

¼ teaspoon pepper

Melt butter in a small saucepan and combine with all other ingredients except lobster. Transfer half of butter mixture to a baking dish and reserve the remaining half. Add lobster tails to the baking dish and cover. Refrigerate 1 to 2 hours but no longer.

Season grill grates; preheat on HI for 5 minutes, then reduce to appropriate cook setting. With sharp knife or cleaver, cut lobster tails in half lengthwise, through shells. Grill, flesh

sides down, about 4 minutes, or until lightly browned. Turn and continue cooking until heated through, 12 to 16 minutes longer, turning every four minutes and basting occasionally with the herbed butter from the baking dish.

Reheat reserved butter mixture to serve with lobster tails as a dipping sauce. *Makes 4 servings*

	Preheat	Setting	Time
Electric	HI	10	16 to 20
Gas	HI	MED	16 to 20

Cajun Salmon

Dry rubs of herbs or spices are one way to add flavor without adding fat. Try this versatile, fiery version on swordfish, chicken, and pork.

1½ teaspoons paprika

½ teaspoon salt

½ teaspoon dried thyme

½ teaspoon dried basil

¼ teaspoon garlic powder

¼ teaspoon onion powder

¼ teaspoon pepper

⅛ teaspoon cayenne pepper, or to taste

4 salmon fillets (6 ounces each), 1-inch thick in center, skin removed

In small bowl, combine all spices and rub mixture into both sides of fish.

Season grill grates; preheat on HI for 5 minutes, then reduce to appropriate cook setting. Grill fish 10 to 20 minutes, or until it flakes easily; turn after half the cooking time.

Makes 4 servings

	Preheat	Setting	Time
Electric	HI	10	10 to 20
Gas	HI	MED	10 to 18

Grilled Trout with Sicilian Spinach Stuffing

If Popeye were Sicilian, this is how he'd cook his spinach. It makes a classic southern Italian stuffing.

¼ cup golden raisins
¼ cup dry white wine
⅓ cup pine nuts
2 tablespoons olive oil, divided
4 garlic cloves, crushed through a press
10 ounces fresh spinach with stems removed, coarsely chopped, or 1 package (10 ounces) frozen chopped spinach, thawed and squeezed dry
¾ teaspoon salt, divided
¾ teaspoon pepper, divided
4 whole rainbow trout (about 1 pound each), cleaned
Lemon wedges, optional

In small bowl, let raisins plump in the wine for 30 minutes; drain and set aside (discard the wine). In medium skillet at setting 6 (for Designer gas model, use MED), toast pine nuts about 6 minutes, stirring often; set aside. Add 1 tablespoon oil and the garlic to skillet, then add the spinach in batches, stirring until first batch wilts before adding the next. (If using frozen spinach, add it all at once.) Mix in raisins and pine nuts. Cook 3 to 4 minutes, or until mixture is heated through. If any liquid remains, drain it by placing mixture in a sieve and pressing with the back of a spoon. Season with ½ teaspoon salt and ½ teaspoon pepper; let cool completely.

Make two shallow diagonal slashes in the thickest part of each trout on both sides. Sprinkle remaining salt and pepper inside trout cavity; divide spinach mixture among the trout, stuffing each with about ⅓ cup filling. Brush trout with remaining olive oil.

Season grill grates; preheat on HI for 5 minutes, then reduce to appropriate cook setting. Place fish diagonally on grill, alternating the direction of heads and tails. Grill 20 to 25 minutes, or until flesh flakes easily with a fork. Turn after half the cooking time, again alternating direction of heads and tails. Serve with lemon wedges, if desired.

Makes 4 servings

	Preheat	Setting	Time
Electric	HI	10	20 to 25
Gas	HI	MED	20 to 25

17

Grilled Vegetables in Chianti-Herb Marinade

Grilled vegetables make a bountiful side dish, or may be served with rice or pasta as a main course. Be sure to cut the vegetables as specified to keep them from falling through the grate during grilling.

I small (about 12 ounces) eggplant, cut lengthwise into six ½-inch slices

1½ teaspoons salt, divided

1 cup Chianti

⅓ cup extra-virgin olive oil

1 tablespoon chopped fresh rosemary, or 1½ teaspoons dried

1 tablespoon chopped fresh thyme, or 1½ teaspoons dried

1 bay leaf, torn in half

2 garlic cloves, minced

¼ teaspoon pepper

2 small zucchini (about 1 pound), cut lengthwise into six ½-inch slices

1 yellow bell pepper, seeded and cut into sixths

1 red bell pepper, seeded and cut into sixths

1 red onion, cut into six wedges, root end left intact

12 green onions, trimmed and cleaned

Balsamic vinegar, optional

Place eggplant slices in a large colander and sprinkle with 1 teaspoon salt. Let stand 1 hour to drain off excess moisture. Rinse slices well under cold running water; drain and pat dry.

Meanwhile, in large bowl, whisk together wine, olive oil, rosemary, thyme, bay leaf, garlic, remaining teaspoon salt, and pepper.

Place all vegetables in marinade. Let stand 1 hour, turning often.

Season grill grates; preheat on HI for 5 minutes. Cook eggplant, zucchini, peppers, and onion in two batches, about 9 to 12 minutes per batch. Turn after half the cooking time and baste often with marinade. Add the green onions during the last 3 to 4 minutes of cooking, turning them once.

To serve, drizzle the hot vegetables with balsamic vinegar if desired.

Makes 6 servings

	Preheat	Setting	Time
Electric	HI	HI	9 to 12
Gas	HI	HI	9 to 12

Grilled Portobello Salad with Tomato Vinaigrette

Portobello mushrooms are a thick, knife-and-fork variety substantial enough to stand in for beef as a hearty first course. You'll love their earthy flavor.

6 portobello mushrooms (about 1½ pounds)

⅔ cup balsamic vinegar

8 garlic cloves, minced

4 tablespoons chopped parsley

1 teaspoon dried oregano

1 teaspoon dried thyme

1⅛ teaspoons salt, divided

⅝ teaspoon freshly ground pepper, divided

1 cup, plus 1 tablespoon, olive oil

2 medium red onions, sliced ½-inch thick

6 small tomatoes (about 1 pound), peeled, seeded, and chopped

6 cups (about two bunches) bitter salad greens, such as arugula or watercress

Snap off the mushroom stems and discard; wipe caps with damp paper towels to remove any grit. Cut mushroom caps into ½-inch-thick slices and set aside.

To make the tomato vinaigrette, combine balsamic vinegar, garlic, parsley, oregano, thyme, 1 teaspoon salt, and ½ teaspoon pepper. Slowly whisk in 1 cup oil in a thin stream. Reserve ½ cup vinaigrette; place mushrooms in bowl

and toss to coat. Cover and set aside to marinate 15 minutes.

Meanwhile, lightly brush onions with remaining olive oil on both sides and season with remaining salt and pepper. Season grill grates; preheat on HI for 5 minutes. Grill onions 10 minutes, or until soft and lightly golden, turning once halfway through cooking time. Remove from grill; let cool. Coarsely chop onions and add to reserved vinaigrette along with chopped tomatoes.

Grill portobellos 4 to 5 minutes, turning halfway through cooking time (cook in batches if necessary to avoid overcrowding the grill). When done, remove from grill and set aside to cool slightly.

Toss the greens with the reserved vinaigrette, onions, and tomatoes; divide among six salad plates. Top greens with mushroom slices and drizzle with any vinaigrette remaining in bowl.

Makes 6 servings

	Preheat	Setting	Time
Electric	HI	HI	14 to 15
Gas	HI	HI	14 to 15

Grilled Eggplant and Mozzarella Sandwiches

Grilled eggplant slices fill in for bread to make these out-of-the-ordinary sandwiches. Choose an elongated eggplant rather than a round, plump one to get as many equally sized slices as possible.

1 large eggplant (about 1¼ pounds)

1 teaspoon salt

3 tablespoons extra-virgin olive oil

1 garlic clove, crushed through a press

½ teaspoon dried oregano

4 ounces mozzarella, thinly sliced, or chevre (goat cheese), crumbled

¼ cup oil-packed sun-dried tomatoes, drained and chopped

2 tablespoons chopped fresh basil

¼ teaspoon crushed red pepper flakes, or to taste

Balsamic vinegar, optional

With serrated knife, cut eggplant crosswise into ¼-inch slices. Use the eight largest slices for this recipe and save remaining eggplant for another

fruit

use. Place slices in a colander and toss well with salt. Let slices stand 1 hour to release bitter flavor, then rinse well under cold running water and pat dry with paper towels. Meanwhile, in small bowl, combine oil, garlic, and oregano; let stand 1 hour.

Season grill grates; preheat on HI for 5 minutes, then reduce to appropriate cook setting.

Brush eggplant slices with herbed olive oil; grill 14 to 16 minutes, or until golden brown and tender, turning halfway through cooking time. When eggplant is cooked, turn the slices again and top four of them with cheese, then sprinkle with sun-dried tomatoes, basil, and crushed red pepper. Stack the remaining eggplant slices on top, hot side facing inward, to form sandwiches. Grill 2 to 4 minutes more or until cheese melts, turning once. Sprinkle with balsamic vinegar if desired.

Makes 4 sandwiches

	Preheat	Setting	Time
Electric	HI	10	16 to 20
Gas	HI	MED	16 to 18

Citrusy Fruit and **Vegetable Kebabs**

This unusual combination of ingredients results in a riot of hot, tangy, and sweet flavors and sensational textures. It's wonderful as a light springtime lunch.

- 2 tablespoons orange juice, preferably fresh-squeezed
- 1 teaspoon minced shallots
- 1 tablespoon each freshly squeezed lemon and lime juice (or use juice of one whole lemon or lime in place of the two different juices)
- 1 teaspoon Dijon mustard
- 4 tablespoons vegetable oil, divided
- 8 bamboo skewers (6-inch size), soaked in water for 30 minutes
- 1 red bell pepper, cut into 16 1-inch squares
- 1 yellow bell pepper, cut into 16 1-inch squares
- 2 small hot chili peppers, cut into 8 pieces
- 1 small pineapple, cut into 1-inch cubes

Citrusy Fruit and Vegetable Kebabs

- 2 kiwifruit, peeled and quartered
- 2 bunches (about 4 cups) watercress, stems removed

To make the citrus vinaigrette, combine orange juice, shallots, lemon juice, lime juice, and mustard in a small bowl. Slowly whisk in 3 tablespoons oil in a thin stream; set aside.

To prepare the fruit kebabs, alternately thread the peppers and fruit onto the skewers, using 2 pieces of red pepper, 2 pieces of yellow pepper, 1 piece of hot chili pepper, 2 chunks of pineapple, and 1 quarter of kiwifruit for each. Leave 1 inch free at one end of each skewer for easier turning on the grill. Brush fruit and peppers with the remaining oil.

Season grill grates; preheat on HI for 5 minutes, then reduce to appropriate cook setting. Grill kebabs 11 to 13 minutes, or until peppers are tender, turning skewers every 3 minutes.

To serve, toss watercress with ¼ cup of the citrus vinaigrette and divide among 4 salad plates. Top each serving with 2 kebabs; drizzle with remaining dressing. *Makes 4 servings*

	Preheat	Setting	Time
Electric	HI	10	11 to 13
Gas	HI	MED	11 to 13

Multi-Grain Buttermilk Pancakes

GRIDDLE

French toast, melt-in-your-mouth sandwiches, homemade pancakes, and even desserts put the griddle accessory to work. Look through these recipes for inspiration, but remember the griddle can also be used for such basics as bacon, eggs, and hash-brown potatoes. For best results with any of these dishes, preheat griddle for five minutes, then reduce heat to the proper cook setting. The griddle's nonstick surface makes turning foods—and cleaning up after them—a breeze. To protect the cooking surface, grease griddle lightly after preheating, and use utensils made for nonstick cooking equipment. In addition, the griddle's unique construction lets excess fats drain away. Remember to clean the grease-collection container often.

...golden brown, turning when bubbles appear and edges look dry. Repeat with remaining batter. Serve hot with butter and maple syrup.

Makes 10 pancakes

Variation 1: To make Apple Pancakes, follow basic recipe but increase sugar to ¼ cup. Add 1 teaspoon ground cinnamon and ¼ teaspoon ground nutmeg to dry ingredients. Stir 1 cup peeled, grated tart apple (such as Granny Smith) into batter.

Makes 12 pancakes

Variation 2: To make Blueberry Pancakes, follow basic recipe but stir 1 cup blueberries, fresh or frozen (thawed and well-drained), and 1 teaspoon grated lemon zest into batter.

Makes 12 pancakes

Variation 3: To make Carrot-Currant Pancakes, follow basic recipe but increase sugar to ¼ cup and add ½ teaspoon ground cinnamon, ½ teaspoon ground allspice, and ¼ teaspoon ground nutmeg to dry ingredients. Stir 1 cup grated carrots and ½ cup dried currants into batter.

Makes 12 pancakes

	Preheat	Setting	Time
Expressions Electric	HI	10	5 to 6
Designer Electric	10	10	5 to 6
Designer Gas	HI	HI	5 to 6

Multi-Grain Buttermilk Pancakes

Here's a great way to get nutritious grains into your diet first thing in the morning. To serve the pancakes all at once, transfer the first batch to a baking sheet and keep warm in a 200° oven.

¾ cup unbleached all-purpose flour
½ cup whole wheat flour
2 tablespoons sugar
1 teaspoon baking powder
1 teaspoon baking soda
¼ teaspoon salt
¼ cup rolled oats
1 cup plus 2 tablespoons
  low-fat buttermilk
3 large eggs, or ¾ cup liquid
  egg substitute
¾ cup (½ stick) melted butter
  or vegetable oil
Butter and maple syrup, optional

Preheat griddle on appropriate setting for 5 minutes, then adjust to cook setting. Into medium bowl, sift flour, whole wheat flour, sugar, baking powder, baking soda, and salt. Stir in oats. Add buttermilk, eggs, and melted butter. Stir mixture only until dry ingredients are moistened.

Pour batter by ⅓ cupfuls onto griddle, forming about 6 pancakes at a time. Cook pancakes until

Three-Vegetable **Pancakes**

These versatile little rounds are great on their own with a side order of greens, but you'll also love them served with your favorite meat.

- 1 large baking potato (about 8 ounces), peeled
- 1 medium onion, peeled
- 1 medium zucchini, scrubbed
- 2 medium carrots, peeled
- 2 large eggs, beaten
- 3 tablespoons all-purpose flour
- 1 teaspoon chopped fresh rosemary, or ½ teaspoon dried
- ½ teaspoon baking powder
- 1 garlic clove, crushed through a press
- 2 teaspoons salt
- 1 teaspoon pepper
- Light sour cream or plain yogurt, optional

Coarsely grate potato, onion, zucchini, and carrots into a medium bowl. Squeeze well to remove as much liquid as possible. You should have about 2½ packed cups of vegetables. Place in medium bowl; add eggs, flour, rosemary, baking powder, garlic, salt, and pepper, and mix well.

Preheat griddle on appropriate setting for 5 minutes, then adjust to cook setting. Drop batter onto griddle, ¼ cup at a time, forming six pancakes. With a nonstick pancake turner, spread mixture out to make 5-inch round pancakes.

Cook until pancakes are set and golden brown, turning after half the time. (For Designer gas model, the first turn will be after 1½ to 2 minutes). Repeat with remaining mixture. Serve with light sour cream or yogurt, if desired.   *Makes 8 to 9 pancakes*

	Preheat	Setting	Time
Expressions Electric	HI	10	3 to 5
Designer Electric	10	10	3 to 5
Designer Gas	HI	HI	2 to 5

Potato and Herb Stuffed **Flatbreads**

These delightfully spicy breads are often served as a side dish in Indian restaurants, but when topped with a dollop of plain yogurt and served with a green salad, they make an excellent light lunch or dinner.

- 1½ cups unbleached all-purpose flour, plus additional flour for kneading
- 1½ cups whole wheat flour
- 3 teaspoons salt, divided
- 5 tablespoons vegetable oil, divided
- 1 cup warm water
- 2 large potatoes (about 1 pound), peeled and boiled until tender
- 4 green onions, white and green parts, minced
- ¼ cup chopped fresh cilantro
- 2 teaspoons ground cumin
- 2 teaspoons ground coriander
- ½ teaspoon cayenne pepper
- ½ cup frozen peas, thawed
- 2 tablespoons butter, melted

To make dough, sift all-purpose flour, whole wheat flour, and 2 teaspoons salt into a large mixing bowl. Make a well in the center of the flour; add 3 tablespoons oil and warm water. Mix, adding more water one tablespoon at a time if necessary, to make a firm dough. Gather dough into a ball; turn onto lightly floured surface and knead 8 to 10 minutes or until smooth and elastic. Cover with a damp towel; let stand 30 minutes.

To make filling, in medium bowl, mash potatoes with a large fork and combine with green onions, cilantro, cumin, coriander, 1 teaspoon salt, and cayenne pepper. Stir in peas.

Divide dough into 10 balls, each approximately 3 inches in diameter. Working with one ball at a time (keep remaining dough under damp towel), roll out into 7-inch rounds. Divide filling, placing 3 to 4 tablespoons in center of each flattened dough round, spreading it into a 4-inch circle. Pull up edges of dough to enclose filling, gently pressing out the air and pinching edges together to seal. Pat the filled dough to make a thick, even patty about 6 inches in diameter. Set

Potato and Herb Stuffed Flatbreads

brunch

prepared rounds aside and keep covered with a damp towel.

Preheat griddle on appropriate setting for 5 minutes. Combine melted butter with the remaining oil; lightly brush on griddle. Place three flatbreads on griddle and cook about 8 minutes, or until the undersides are lightly browned. Brush tops of dough rounds with remaining butter and oil; turn carefully and cook about 4 minutes, or until the other side is browned. Repeat with remaining dough rounds, cooking up to three at a time. Serve warm.

Breads can be reheated on the griddle for a minute or so before serving.   *Makes 10 flatbreads*

	Preheat	Setting	Time
Expressions Electric	HI	10	12
Designer Electric	9	9	12
Designer Gas	MED	MED	12

Stuffed **French Toast**

Indulge your sweet tooth at Sunday brunch with this slightly sinful chocolate-stuffed French toast sandwich.

3 large eggs
½ cup half-and-half
2 tablespoons sugar
8 slices firm white or egg (challah) bread
4 ounces milk chocolate, finely chopped (use food processor fitted with steel blade)
½ cup maple syrup
½ teaspoon grated orange zest

Preheat griddle on appropriate setting for 5 minutes. In shallow bowl, blend eggs, half-and-half, and sugar. Dip 4 bread slices in egg mixture, turning to coat both sides. Place bread on griddle and cook about 2 minutes, or until bottoms are golden. Turn the slices over and sprinkle 2 of them with half of the chocolate. Cook about 2 minutes more, then top the melted chocolate slices with the 2 remaining plain slices to form a sandwich. If necessary, carefully turn sandwiches again to obtain a uniform golden color and melt the chocolate thoroughly. Repeat with remaining bread and chocolate.

In small saucepan, combine maple syrup and orange zest; heat on a low setting for about 5 minutes, or until mixture is warmed through. Pour into a sauceboat and serve on the side.   *Makes 4 servings*

	Preheat	Setting	Time
Expressions Electric	HI	10	5 to 7
Designer Electric	10	10	4 to 6
Designer Gas	HI	HI	4 to 7

Asparagus and Ham **Mini-Omelets**

From China to Korea, Asian cooks love to prepare vegetable omelets like this one. Served with a savory dipping sauce, the egg patties make a delicious brunch, lunch, or supper entrée.

¼ cup soy sauce
¼ cup rice vinegar
2 tablespoons sesame oil
1 fresh hot chili pepper, cut into thin rounds, optional
1 tablespoon vegetable oil
1 cup (about ½ pound) asparagus spears, chopped into ¼-inch pieces
2 green onions, white and green parts, chopped
1 garlic clove, minced
1 tablespoon water
2 ounces smoked ham, chopped
4 large eggs
¼ teaspoon salt
¼ teaspoon pepper

To make dipping sauce, combine soy sauce, rice vinegar, sesame oil, and chili pepper. Set aside.

To make omelets, preheat griddle on appropriate setting for 5 minutes, then reduce to cook setting. Spread vegetable oil on griddle and place asparagus, green onions, and garlic on top; sprinkle with water. Cook 4 to 5 minutes, or until asparagus is tender-crisp, turning occasionally. Add ham and cook 1 minute longer. Transfer mixture to plate and let cool to lukewarm.

In medium bowl, whisk together eggs, salt, and pepper. Pour egg mixture by ¼ cupfuls, two at a time, onto griddle. Place about ¼ cup of the vegetable mix-

ture in the center of each egg circle; using a nonstick pancake turner, pull the edges of the cooked eggs up over vegetables to form patties. Cook about 2 minutes, or until eggs are set, turning carefully after half the time. Repeat with remaining ingredients. Serve with individual bowls of sauce for dipping.   *Makes 4 servings*

	Preheat	Setting	Time
Expressions Electric	HI	7	7 to 9
Designer Electric	7	7	7 to 9
Designer Gas	MED	MED	7 to 8

Seasoned **Hash Browns**

This is the classic side order for a hearty bacon-and-egg breakfast. Pass the ketchup—it's the traditional topping.

2 pounds white potatoes (about 6 medium), pared
¼ cup onion, minced
1 teaspoon garlic salt
½ teaspoon fennel seed, optional
⅛ teaspoon pepper
3 tablespoons butter or margarine

Shred potatoes into large bowl of ice water. Drain potatoes, pressing out excess moisture. Transfer to large mixing bowl. Blend in onion, garlic salt, fennel seed, and pepper. Mix well. Set aside.

Preheat griddle on appropriate setting for five minutes, then adjust to cook setting. Melt butter on griddle, spreading over surface as it melts. Spread potatoes to within ½ inch of sides and 1½ inches of ends. With pancake turner, gently press down potatoes. Fry potatoes 12 to 15 minutes, or until set and golden brown. With edge of pancake turner, carefully cut potatoes into 6 equal portions. Turn each portion. Cook potatoes 8 to 10 minutes longer, or until golden brown and fork tender.

Makes 6 servings

	Preheat	Setting	Time
Expressions Electric	HI	8	20 to 25
Designer Electric	8	8	20 to 25
Designer Gas	MED	MED	20 to 25

23

Southwestern Corncakes

Smoked Turkey Monte Cristo **Sandwiches**

The smoked versions of Gouda and mozzarella give these usually mild-mannered cheeses a big flavor boost, particularly when combined with smoked turkey. This egg-dipped hot sandwich is a sure-fire favorite.

8 slices home-style white or whole-grain bread
4 teaspoons Dijon mustard
8 ounces sliced smoked turkey
4 ounces smoked Gouda or smoked mozzarella cheese, sliced
2 large eggs
½ cup milk
Generous pinch of salt
Pinch of pepper
Butter for greasing griddle

Preheat griddle on appropriate setting for 5 minutes. Spread four of the bread slices with mustard, layer smoked turkey and cheese on top; place remaining four bread slices over each to make sandwiches. In a 9-inch pie plate, whisk together eggs, milk, salt, and pepper. Dip sandwiches in egg mixture, turning to coat both sides.

Lightly grease griddle with butter. Place sandwiches, cheese-side down, on griddle; cook 4 to 9 minutes or until golden brown, turning every 2 minutes.   Makes 4 sandwiches

	Preheat	Setting	Time
Expressions Electric	HI	10	7 to 9
Designer Electric	9	9	5 to 7
Designer Gas	HI	HI	4 to 6

Apple, Brie, and Pecan **Quesadillas**

This elegant combination of French, American, and Mexican cuisines makes a deliciously simple appetizer.

6 flour tortillas (6-inch size)
4 ounces firm brie, including rind, shredded (place cheese in freezer for 15 minutes for easier shredding)
⅓ cup pecans, chopped
1 medium tart apple (such as Granny Smith), peeled, cored, and grated

Preheat griddle on appropriate setting for 5 minutes, then adjust to cook setting.

Place three tortillas on griddle and sprinkle each with cheese, nuts, and grated apple, divided evenly. Top each with another tortilla. Cook 4 minutes or until cheese melts, turning after 2 minutes. Cut each quesadilla into six wedges; serve warm.   Makes 18 appetizers

	Preheat	Setting	Time
Expressions Electric	HI	10	4
Designer Electric	9	9	4
Designer Gas	MED	MED	4

Southwestern **Corncakes**

This versatile recipe can be used to form party-sized fare, or you can measure batter to make larger pancakes.

½ cup yellow cornmeal
2 tablespoons all-purpose flour
½ teaspoon baking soda
¼ teaspoon salt
⅛ teaspoon cayenne pepper
1 tablespoon canola oil
¾ cup buttermilk
2 large eggs, lightly beaten
1 cup corn kernels, thawed if frozen, drained if canned
¼ cup grated Monterey Jack cheese
¼ cup finely diced red bell pepper
2 green onions, thinly sliced
2 tablespoons chopped cilantro
1 small hot chili pepper, minced

In medium bowl, combine cornmeal, flour, baking soda, salt, and cayenne pepper. Stir in canola oil, buttermilk, and eggs just until combined. Fold in corn, cheese, bell pepper, green onions, cilantro, and chili pepper.

Preheat griddle at appropriate setting for 5 minutes, then adjust to cook setting. Drop batter onto griddle by ¼ cupfuls to make pancakes; cook 3 to 4 minutes, or until golden, turning

after half the cooking time. Repeat with remaining batter. To make appetizer-size corncakes, drop batter onto griddle by spoonfuls and adjust cooking times to 2 to 3 minutes.
  Makes 12 pancakes or 4 dozen appetizers

	Preheat	Setting	Time
Expressions Electric	HI	10	3 to 4
Designer Electric	10	10	3 to 4
Designer Gas	HI	HI	3 to 4

Grilled Cheddar and Apple **Sandwiches**

Crisp apple slices complement sharp cheddar cheese in this tasty grilled sandwich. Try the apple butter–mustard spread on turkey and ham sandwiches, too.

2 tablespoons apple butter
2 tablespoons Dijon mustard
8 slices whole wheat bread
Softened butter or margarine
4 ounces sharp cheddar cheese, shredded
1 tart apple (such as Granny Smith), cored and cut into ⅛-inch slices

In small bowl, combine apple butter and mustard; spread one side of each bread slice with the mixture, and one side with butter. With buttered sides facing out, fill each sandwich with shredded cheese and apple slices, dividing evenly.

Preheat griddle on appropriate setting for 5 minutes, then adjust to cook setting. Cook sandwiches 4 to 7 minutes, or until cheese melts and bread is golden brown. Turn every 1½ to 2 minutes.   Makes 4 sandwiches

	Preheat	Setting	Time
Expressions Electric	HI	10	5 to 7
Designer Electric	9	9	5 to 7
Designer Gas	HI	HI	4 to 6

Grilled Tuna Sandwiches
with Vegetable Slaw

Thick-cut tuna has a steaklike appeal; topped with colorful shredded vegetables and served on crusty bread, this sandwich makes a satisfying meal.

- ⅓ cup chopped fresh basil, or a combination of ⅓ cup fresh parsley, chopped, and 1 teaspoon dried basil
- 3 tablespoons freshly squeezed lemon juice
- 1 tablespoon Dijon mustard
- 2 cloves garlic, divided, crushed through a press
- ¼ cup olive oil
- ¼ teaspoon crushed hot red pepper flakes
- 4 tuna steaks (about 1¼ pounds), cut 1-inch thick
- 3 tablespoons red wine vinegar
- 1 teaspoon celery seeds
- 1 teaspoon salt
- ¼ teaspoon pepper
- ½ cup olive oil
- 8 ounces (about 3 cups) shredded green cabbage
- 1 medium carrot, peeled and shredded
- 1 red bell pepper, seeded and cut into very thin strips
- ¼ cup chopped parsley
- 4 French or Italian rolls, split
- 2 tablespoons regular or low-fat mayonnaise

To make the marinade, combine basil, lemon juice, mustard, 1 clove garlic, olive oil, and red pepper in a blender or food processor and blend until smooth; pour into a baking dish and add the tuna steak. Cover dish and refrigerate 1 to 2 hours, but no longer, turning fish occasionally.

To make the vegetable slaw, in large bowl, whisk together the vinegar, celery seeds, remaining garlic, salt, and pepper Gradually whisk in oil. Add cabbage, carrot, bell pepper, and parsley; toss well. Cover and refrigerate at least 2 hours.

Season grill grates; preheat on HI for 5 minutes, then reduce to appropriate cook setting. Cook fish 20 to 25 minutes, or until it reaches desired doneness (140° to 145°). Turn after half the cooking time. Toast rolls on the grill during the last 4 minutes of cooking time.

To serve, spread toasted rolls with mayonnaise. Place one tuna steak on each roll and top with ¼ cup of the vegetable slaw. Serve remaining slaw on the side.

Makes 4 sandwiches

	Preheat	Setting	Time
Expressions Electric	HI	10	20 to 25
Designer Electric	HI	10	20 to 25
Designer Gas	HI	MED	20 to 25

New Cuban Sandwiches

This is a time-honored favorite in Hispanic communities throughout the country. It is usually made with roast pork, but lean, boneless pork tenderloin slices cook quickly on the griddle—and they're more slimming.

- 1 tablespoon olive oil, plus additional oil for grilling
- 1 teaspoon dried oregano
- 1 garlic clove, crushed through a press
- 2 teaspoons salt
- ¼ teaspoon pepper
- 12 ounces pork tenderloin, cut crosswise into ¼-inch slices
- 1 tablespoon regular or low-fat mayonnaise
- 1 tablespoon Dijon mustard
- 4 French rolls, split
- 8 ounces thin-sliced ham or salami, cut to fit French rolls
- 8 ounces thin-sliced Swiss cheese, cut to fit French rolls
- 12 sour dill pickle slices

In medium bowl, combine oil, oregano, garlic, salt, and pepper. Add pork slices and toss well to coat. Cover and refrigerate for 1 to 6 hours.

Preheat griddle on appropriate setting for 5 minutes; cook pork slices 2 to 5 minutes, or until cooked through, turning after first minute or two (on Designer models, cook on preheat setting; on Expressions model, cook on setting 10). Set aside. Reduce heat to sandwich setting.

In small bowl, combine mayonnaise and mustard; spread inside French rolls. Divide pork slices among the rolls. Top with ham, cheese, and pickles. Place tops of rolls on filling and press down firmly.

Lightly grease griddle with olive oil. Place sandwiches close together, but not touching, on griddle. Weigh down sandwiches with a heavy cast-iron pan or a large baking dish filled with cans. Cook the sandwiches about 8 minutes (9 minutes on Expressions model), or until undersides are crisp. Turn sandwiches and cook until the other sides are golden brown and the cheese is completely melted, two to three minutes more.

Makes 4 sandwiches

	Preheat	Setting	Time
Expressions Electric	HI	10	11 to 13
Designer Electric	9	9	12 to 13
Designer Gas	HI	HI	10 to 12

Chili-Bean Burgers

Here's a neatly packaged version of a family favorite. It's got everything regular chili has, but it all shapes up in burger form.

- 1 tablespoon olive oil
- 1 small onion, finely chopped
- 1 garlic clove, minced
- 1 pound lean ground beef
- 1 cup canned black beans, rinsed and drained
- 1 tablespoon chili powder
- ½ teaspoon ground cumin
- ¾ teaspoon salt
- 6 hamburger buns, split and toasted on griddle, if desired
- 6 slices ripe tomato, about ½-inch thick
- Ketchup or barbecue sauce, optional

In small skillet, heat oil at setting 6 or 7 (for Designer gas model, use MED). Add onion and garlic; cook 5 minutes or until softened. Set aside to cool slightly.

In medium bowl, combine ground beef, beans, onion and garlic mixture, chili powder, cumin, and salt. Shape into 6 burgers, each ½- to ¾-inch thick.

Preheat griddle on appropriate setting for 5 minutes. Cook burgers 7 to 11 minutes, or until they're done but still juicy, turning after half the cooking time.

To serve, place burgers on buns and top with tomato slices and condiments, if desired.

Makes 6 servings

	Preheat	Setting	Time
Expressions Electric	HI	HI	7 to 10
Designer Electric	9	9	7 to 11
Designer Gas	MED	MED	7 to 10

Chili-Bean Burgers

Turkey-Salsa **Burgers**

Turkey keeps these burgers light: salsa keeps them juicy. If you prefer, you can make these tangy patties with ground chicken breast.

1 ripe avocado, pitted and chopped

¼ cup prepared salsa, plus ¾ cup more, well drained (about ½ cup after draining)

¼ cup regular or nonfat sour cream

1 small hot chili pepper, seeded and minced

1 pound ground turkey or ground chicken breast

1 teaspoon salt

½ teaspoon freshly ground pepper

Vegetable oil

4 slices red onion, sliced ¼-inch thick

4 hamburger buns, split and toasted on griddle, if desired

To make the salsa, in small bowl, combine the avocado, ¼ cup prepared salsa, sour cream, and chili pepper; mix thoroughly, cover, and refrigerate until ready to serve.

To make the burgers, in a medium bowl, combine the ground turkey or chicken breast with the drained salsa, salt, and pepper. Divide mixture and shape into four burgers, each ½- to ¾-inch thick.

Preheat griddle on the appropriate setting for 5 minutes; lightly grease with vegetable oil. Cook burgers and onion slices 9 to 12 minutes, or until the meat is cooked through but still juicy and the onions are tender and brown. Turn after half the cooking time. If desired, place buns on griddle during last 3 minutes of burger cooking time to toast.

To serve, top burgers with salsa and place in toasted buns. **Makes 4 servings**

	Preheat	Setting	Time
Expressions Electric	HI	HI	9 to 11
Designer Electric	9	9	10 to 12
Designer Gas	MED	MED	10 to 12

Chicken and Asparagus Melt with Salsa Verde

Salsa verde is a cool, refreshing condiment that complements many Italian meat dishes. For a twist, place thinly sliced prosciutto inside the chicken breasts before adding asparagus.

½ cup fresh parsley, chopped

¼ cup fresh basil, chopped

¼ cup slivered almonds

1 tablespoon Dijon mustard

1 tablespoon freshly squeezed lemon juice

2 anchovy filets, chopped

3 garlic cloves, minced

½ teaspoon pepper, divided

½ cup virgin olive oil, divided

4 skinless, boneless chicken breasts, about 6 ounces each

¼ teaspoon salt

4 ounces fontina, mozzarella, or Gruyère cheese, grated

8 asparagus spears, peeled and trimmed to fit chicken breasts, partly cooked until crisp-tender

To make the salsa verde, in blender or food processor, combine parsley, basil, almonds, mustard, lemon juice, anchovies, garlic, and ¼ teaspoon pepper. While machine is running, gradually add ½ cup oil and mix until smooth. Transfer to a small bowl; cover and refrigerate until serving.

Place chicken breasts flat on a work surface. Holding a knife parallel to work surface, make an incision along outer edge of each breast and cut toward the center of the meat without separating. Open chicken breasts out like a book. Place meat between two sheets of wax paper or plastic wrap and pound gently to uniform thickness. Season meat inside with salt and remaining pepper. Divide cheese and sprinkle over one half of each open chicken breast. Place 2 asparagus spears on top of cheese and fold meat over to enclose filling.

Preheat griddle on appropriate setting for 5 minutes, then adjust to cook setting. Lightly grease griddle and brush chicken breasts with remaining olive oil. Cook chicken about 2 minutes, or until underside is golden brown; turn. Cook until remaining side of chicken is golden brown and cheese is melted, about 9 minutes more, turning every 2 minutes. To serve, top with salsa verde. **Makes 4 servings**

	Preheat	Setting	Time
Expressions Electric	HI	10	11 to 13
Designer Electric	10	10	11 to 13
Designer Gas	MED	MED	11 to 13

Seared Scallops with Wilted Spinach and Hot Curry Vinaigrette

This sophisticated salad, with its interesting textures and exotic dressing, makes an elegant first course or luncheon entrée. Large sea scallops are easier to prepare than the smaller bay variety.

¾ cup vegetable oil, divided

2 tablespoons shallots or green onions, white part only, minced

1 tablespoon grated fresh ginger

1 garlic clove, minced

1 teaspoon curry powder

½ teaspoon sugar

¼ cup cider vinegar

¾ teaspoon salt, divided

⅛ teaspoon cayenne pepper, or to taste

1 tablespoon olive oil

1½ pounds sea scallops, tendons removed, patted dry with paper towels (if scallops are very large, cut in half crosswise)

½ teaspoon white pepper

1 pound fresh spinach, tough stems removed, well-rinsed and dried

To make the hot curry vinaigrette, in medium saucepan, heat 1 tablespoon vegetable oil at setting 6 (for Designer gas model, use MED). Add shallots and ginger and cook about 2 minutes, or until softened. Add garlic, curry powder, and sugar; stir for 30 seconds. Add cider vinegar and bring to a simmer. Add the remaining vegetable oil and heat through, about 2 minutes; whisk in ½ teaspoon salt and cayenne pepper.

Preheat griddle on appropriate setting for 5 minutes. Lightly grease griddle with olive oil. Season scallops with remaining salt and white pepper; place on griddle and cook 3 to 6 minutes, or until golden brown, turning continuously with kitchen tongs. Do not overcook scallops.

In large mixing bowl, drizzle the warm vinaigrette over spinach and toss to combine. To serve, divide spinach among 4 large dinner plates and arrange scallops on top. Serve immediately.   Makes 4 servings

	Preheat	Setting	Time
Expressions Electric	HI	HI	5 to 6
Designer Electric	10	10	3 to 6
Designer Gas	HI	HI	3 to 6

Parmesan Polenta with Wild Mushroom Ragout

Here's a hearty appetizer that is also delicious as a main course. Polenta can also be topped with your favorite Italian tomato-meat sauce, or served as a side dish for roasts and chops.

1 ounce dried mushrooms, such as porcini or Polish black

6 cups water, divided

2 teaspoons salt, divided

1½ cups stone-ground yellow cornmeal

1 cup (4 ounces) freshly grated Parmesan cheese

3 tablespoons olive oil, divided

1 small onion, chopped

1 garlic clove, minced

2 pounds assorted fresh mushrooms, such as shiitake or portobello (stems removed), crimini, oyster, and white button, in any combination, cut into ½-inch thick slices

¾ cup low-sodium chicken or beef broth (add 1 cup additional stock if not using dried mushrooms)

⅓ cup red wine

¼ cup oil-packed sun-dried tomatoes, drained and chopped

2 tablespoons fresh rosemary, chopped, or 1½ teaspoons dried

½ teaspoon salt

¼ teaspoon pepper

2 tablespoons butter, melted

Place dried mushrooms in a small bowl and add 1 cup boiling water. Let stand about 30 minutes, or until mushrooms are soft. Remove mushrooms from liquid and rinse quickly under cold water to remove grit; chop and set aside. Reserve soaking liquid by lining a mesh strainer or sieve with paper towels and then straining.

To make the polenta, in a heavy bottomed medium saucepan, bring 5 cups water to a boil. Add 1½ teaspoons salt. Using a long-handled wooden spoon, gradually whisk in cornmeal. Reduce heat and cook, stirring constantly, about 25 minutes, or until mixture is thick and smooth. Stir in Parmesan. Spread the polenta in a lightly greased 9-by-5-inch loaf pan. Let stand about 2 hours, or until completely cooled. Cover and refrigerate for 2 hours to set until firm.

To make ragout, in large skillet, heat 1 tablespoon oil at setting 6 (for Designer gas model, use MED). Add onion and garlic and cook 4 to 5 minutes, or until onion is golden. Add the fresh mushrooms, stir, and cover. Cook 8 to 10 minutes, stirring occasionally, until mushrooms release their liquid. Add soaked mushrooms and their reserved liquid, as well as broth, wine, sun-dried tomatoes, rosemary, salt, and pepper. Increase heat to HI and bring to a boil. Reduce to setting 6 (for Designer gas model, use MED) and simmer 6 to 8 minutes or until cooking liquid is reduced to a scant cup. Keep the ragout warm.

Remove polenta from the mold and cut it into twelve squares. In a small bowl, combine melted butter and remaining olive oil.

Preheat griddle on appropriate setting for 5 minutes; grease with butter and oil mixture. Place six slices of the polenta on griddle; brush tops with butter and oil mixture and cook 6 to 10 minutes, or until golden brown, turning after half the time. Repeat with the remaining polenta slices. Serve two slices of polenta per person, topping each serving with about 1 cup of the mushroom ragout.   Makes 6 servings

	Preheat	Setting	Time
Expressions Electric	HI	10	8 to 10
Designer Electric	9	9	8 to 10
Designer Gas	HI	HI	6 to 10

Chocolate Crepes with Caramel Bananas

The secret to light and fluffy crepes is good old-fashioned seltzer. If bananas aren't your favorite fruit, try this lovely hot dessert with peaches and raspberries instead.

1 cup all-purpose flour

¼ cup, plus 1 tablespoon, sugar

2 tablespoons cocoa powder

½ teaspoon salt

2 eggs, beaten

½ cup milk

½ cup seltzer or club soda

¼ cup prepared caramel sauce

1 tablespoon butter

3 finely chopped bananas, or 2½ cups chopped fresh peaches combined with ½ cup fresh raspberries

¼ teaspoon cinnamon

In medium bowl, combine flour, ¼ cup sugar, cocoa powder, and salt. Stir in eggs, milk, and seltzer; set aside 1 hour. Strain batter through a sieve to remove any lumps.

Preheat griddle at appropriate setting for 5 minutes. Drop batter onto griddle by scant ¼ cupfuls into two 6- or 7-inch circles. Repeat, making two crepes at a time. Cook 1½ minutes, then turn and cook 1½ minutes more. Remove and repeat with remaining batter, stacking crepes on a plate until you're ready to use them.

In a small saucepan, heat caramel sauce on LO until warmed through. Melt butter on griddle and add fruit; sprinkle with remaining sugar and cinnamon. Using a nonstick spatula, stir mixture until bananas are warmed through and slightly soft, about 2 minutes. Transfer to a bowl.

Working quickly, while crepes and fruit are still warm, place one crepe on a work surface, smooth side down, and fill with 2 tablespoons of the fruit filling. Roll up to enclose filling and transfer to a dessert plate, seam-side down. Repeat, placing two crepes on each plate. To serve, drizzle with the hot caramel sauce. **Makes 6 servings**

Pineapple Sundaes with Honey-Rum Sauce

	Preheat	Setting	Time
Expressions Electric	HI	9	3
Designer Electric	8	8	3
Designer Gas	MED	MED	3

Pineapple Sundaes with Honey-Rum Sauce

This dessert is dazzling, yet simple to make. For best results, use fresh, juicy pineapple rings; the canned version will have a slightly different texture.

⅓ cup honey

⅓ cup dark rum

3 tablespoons, plus ½ teaspoon, butter

6 fresh pineapple slices, cut about ½-inch thick, core removed

1 quart vanilla ice cream or nonfat frozen yogurt

In small saucepan, bring honey and rum to a simmer on setting 3 or 4 (for Designer gas model, use MED or LO).

Remove from heat and stir in 3 tablespoons butter. Set aside.

Preheat griddle to appropriate setting for 5 minutes, then adjust to cook setting. Lightly grease griddle with ½ teaspoon butter. Place pineapple slices on griddle. Brush tops lightly with sauce, and immediately turn slices over, cooking sauce-side down 3 to 6 minutes. Turn slices once or twice, brushing tops with sauce before each turn. Pineapple should be glazed and golden brown. Transfer slices to a cutting board and chop coarsely.

Spoon ice cream or yogurt into dessert bowls; top with the chopped pineapple and drizzle with remaining sauce. **Makes 6 servings**

	Preheat	Setting	Time
Expressions Electric	HI	10	6
Designer Electric	10	10	6
Designer Gas	HI	HI	3

The classic techniques of rotisserie cooking and steaming are effortless with the rotiss-kebab and cooker-steamer units. The motor-driven rotiss-kebab fits directly over your Expressions or Designer Line electric grill for moister-than-ever, self-basting roasts and poultry. The ample cooker-steamer's two-position wire basket fits the Designer electric model for perfectly steamed vegetables, fish, and seafood. Simply remove the basket to prepare long-simmered, satisfying stews. To see how great these units can be, start with these easy yet deliciously inventive recipes.

Tuscan Pork Arista

Here's a deceptively simple way to roast a pork loin: Cover it with a fragrant herb paste and the meat becomes infused with the flavor as it cooks.

- 2 tablespoons olive oil
- 2 tablespoons chopped fresh rosemary, or 1 tablespoon dried
- Grated zest of 1 lemon
- 2 garlic cloves, minced
- ½ teaspoon salt
- ¼ teaspoon pepper
- 1 boneless pork loin roast (about 2 pounds), trimmed and tied every 2 inches

In a small bowl, mix oil, rosemary, lemon zest, garlic, salt, and pepper to form a paste. With a knife, make six deep incisions in roast. Using your fingers, stuff some of the herb paste into each incision; rub the remainder all over into roast. Wrap meat in plastic wrap and refrigerate 6 hours or overnight.

Unwrap pork roast and center meat on rotisserie spit by spearing and securing with meat holders. Check to see that the roast is balanced properly by holding the spit and rotating it across both palms. Insert spit into motor and center roast over heating element. Plug in rotisserie motor and turn heat to cook setting. Roast pork 35 to 40 minutes per pound, or until a meat thermometer reads 155° (turn off heat and rotisserie motor before inserting thermometer). Remove meat from spit and let stand 10 to 15 minutes until roast reaches 160° before slicing. **Makes 6 to 8 servings**

	Setting	Time
Designer Electric	10	35 to 45 per pound
Expressions Electric	HI	35 to 45 per pound

Roast Duck with Spiced Honey and Cognac Glaze

Sweet glazes are particularly well-suited to dark-meat fowl like duck. You car also use this glaze on Cornish hens with great success.

- 1 duck (5 to 6 pounds), rinsed and patted dry
- ½ teaspoon salt
- ¼ teaspoon freshly ground pepper
- ¼ cup honey
- 2 tablespoons cognac or brandy
- Grated zest of 1 orange
- ¼ teaspoon ground allspice
- Dash of ground cloves

Remove giblets and neck from duck. Rinse and drain duck, and prick or score skin to allow fat to drain properly. Remove excess fat. Season duck inside and out with salt and pepper. Truss the bird with kitchen twine, tying legs and wings close to the body at intervals to make sure it stays compact.

Center duck on rotisserie spit by spearing and securing it with meat holders. Check to see that it is balanced properly by holding the spit and

Tuscan Pork Arista

rotating it in both palms. Insert spit into motor and center duck over heating element. (Note: Empty grease container prior to cooking the duck.) Plug in rotisserie motor and turn heat to HI.

In small bowl, mix honey, cognac, orange zest, allspice, and cloves. During the last 20 minutes of roasting, brush duck occasionally with glaze.

Roast the duck for 90 to 100 minutes, or until a meat thermometer inserted in the thickest part of the meat reads 170° to 185°, depending on desired doneness (turn off the heat and rotisserie motor before inserting thermometer). Remove duck from spit and let stand for 10 to 15 minutes before carving.   *Makes 2 to 4 servings*

	Setting	Time
Designer Electric	HI	90 to 100
Expressions Electric	HI	110 to 140

Contemporary Clambake
with Garlic Mayonnaise

Shellfish lovers will delight in this treat from the sea. To lighten up on the traditional aioli (garlic mayonnaise), replace egg yolks with liquid egg substitute.

- 3 cups dry white wine or lager beer, or 1½ cups of either combined with 1½ cups water
- 1 medium onion, chopped
- 1 tablespoon butter
- ¼ teaspoon dried thyme
- 1 teaspoon salt, divided
- ¼ teaspoon freshly ground pepper
- 6 small red potatoes (about 12 ounces), scrubbed and cut into halves or quarters
- ¼ cup liquid egg substitute
- 2 tablespoons freshly squeezed lemon juice
- 1 teaspoon Dijon mustard
- 1 garlic clove (or more to taste) crushed through a press
- ¼ teaspoon cayenne pepper
- ⅛ teaspoon crushed saffron, optional
- ¼ cup canola oil
- ¼ cup olive oil
- 2 ears corn, husked and cut into 1-inch rounds

- 2 dozen littleneck clams, well scrubbed
- 1 dozen mussels, well scrubbed and debearded
- Lemon wedges, optional
- French or Italian bread

Combine the wine, beer, or mixture with onion, butter, thyme, ½ teaspoon salt, and pepper in bottom section of cooker-steamer unit; bring to a boil. Place potatoes in cooker-steamer basket and insert, with handles up for stewing. Cover and cook on HI for about 15 minutes, or until potatoes are almost tender, turning them halfway through cooking time.

Meanwhile, make the aioli. Pour the liquid egg substitute into a small metal bowl, place in a larger bowl containing hot water, and let stand 5 minutes to remove chill. Pour into blender container and add the lemon juice, mustard, garlic, ½ teaspoon salt, cayenne pepper, and the saffron, if desired. With the blender running, gradually add the oils and blend until the mixture is thick and smooth. Transfer the aioli to two small serving dishes.

Arrange corn around potatoes in the steamer basket. Change handles to locked-down position, then place clams on top of both; steam 6 to 7 minutes. Add mussels and steam until clams and mussels open, about 3 minutes more. If liquid begins to evaporate, reduce cook setting to 8. Discard any shellfish that do not open during cooking. Transfer shellfish, potatoes, and corn to deep soup bowls. Ladle some of the broth over each. Serve with lemon wedges and bread, with aioli on the side for dipping.   *Makes 2 servings*

	Preheat	Setting	Time
Designer Electric	HI	HI	24 to 26

Contemporary Clambake with Garlic Mayonnaise

INDEX

■ GRILL ● GRIDDLE ▲ ROTISS-KEBAB ☆ COOKER-STEAMER